Media Literacy for Kids

Learning About Ads

by Martha E. H. Rustad

Consulting Editor: Gail Saunders-Smith, PhD

Consultant: JoAnne DeLurey Reed
Librarian and Teacher, Scroggins Elementary School
Houston, Texas

CAPSTONE PRESS
a capstone imprint

Pebble Plus is published by Capstone Press,
1710 Roe Crest Drive, North Mankato, Minnesota 56003
www.capstonepub.com

Library of Congress Cataloging-in-Publication Data
Rustad, Martha E. H. (Martha Elizabeth Hillman), 1975–
 Learning about ads / by Martha E.H. Rustad.
    pages cm.—(Pebble plus. Media literacy for kids)
 Includes bibliographical references and index.
 ISBN 978-1-4914-1830-7 (library binding)—ISBN 978-1-4914-1835-2 (ebook pdf)
 1. Advertising—Juvenile literature. 2. Media literacy—Juvenile literature. I. Title.
 HF5829.R87 2015
 659.1—dc23   2014023676

Editorial Credits
Erika L. Shores, editor; Sarah Bennett, designer; Gene Bentdahl, production specialist

Photo Credits
Capstone, cover (back); Capstone Studio: Karon Dubke, 5, 9 (right), 11, 17, 21, cover (front);
Shutterstock: charles taylor, 7 (inset), Donnay Style, 9 (left), egg design, 21 (inset), Juliana
Villalobos, 21 (inset, background), Leonard Zhukovsky, 19, Levent Konuk, 7, Michael
Schneidmiller, 13 (TV), Syda Productions, 13 (inset), Thomas Klee, 22; The Kobal
Collection: AMERICAN IDOL PROD./19 TELEVISION/FOX TV NETWORK/
FREMANTLE MEDIA NORTH AMERICA, 15

Note to Parents and Teachers

The Media Literacy for Kids set supports Common Core State
Standards related to language arts. This book describes and illustrates
advertisements and their purpose. The images support early readers
in understanding the text. The repetition of words and phrases helps
early readers learn new words. This book also introduces early readers
to subject-specific vocabulary words, which are defined in the Glossary
section. Early readers may need assistance to read some words and to
use the Table of Contents, Glossary, Read More, Internet Sites, Critical
Thinking Using the Common Core, and Index sections of the book.

Printed in the United States of America in Stevens Point, Wisconsin.
092014   008479WZS15

Table of Contents

Ads Sell

Buy this toy! Ask for that cereal!
Ads tell people to buy things.
Companies use ads to show
what they sell.

Ad is short for advertisement.

THIS WEEK ONLY!

On Sale No...

...one get...

Ads target certain buyers. Toy ads run during kids' TV shows. Toy companies know kids see the ads. They hope kids will ask for the toys.

Ads sometimes use tricks. People in ads act excited. Products look better than they really are. These tricks work when people buy the items.

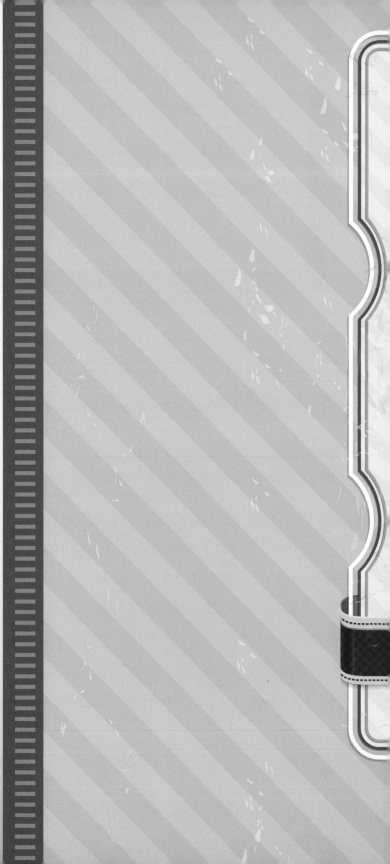

Ads Everywhere

Some ads are printed on paper.

Print ads are in newspapers

and magazines.

Businesses send print ads

in the mail.

Commercials play during

TV shows and online.

They use actors to sell products.

Companies want people to

remember their commercials.

13

Actors might use certain products in shows or movies. A company pays for the product to be seen in the TV show or movie. This product placement is a kind of ad.

Coca-Cola paid to have judges use cups with its logo during the TV show *American Idol*.

Where else do you see ads?

Ads are on city buses.

Billboards line roads.

Even clothes show the company

that made them.

Be Aware of Ads

Be aware of ads all around you.

Ads are always selling.

So think carefully before buying.

HEART POINTS

You need more
Heart Points
to win!

CLICK HERE TO BUY
500 Heart Points
Only $1.99!

21

Activity: Make an Ad

Make up an ad for your favorite fruit. Try to convince your audience to like the fruit too.

What You Do

1. Think about your favorite fruit. Is it sweet, crunchy, and juicy? What else makes it your favorite? Is it easy to peel and eat?

2. Write an ad. Tell readers why your fruit is best. Use words like "best," "yummy," "delicious," and "love."

3. Draw pictures of people eating the fruit. Use bright colors, glitter, stickers, and other things to draw attention to your ad.

4. Ask friends, classmates, or family members to look at your ad. What about the ad makes them want to eat the fruit?

What You Need

paper

crayons or markers

glitter, stickers, or other decorations

Glossary

ad—a notice that calls attention to a product or an event; ad is short for advertisement

billboard—a large sign beside a road on which a company or business advertises

commercial—an ad that plays during breaks in TV shows

product—something a business is selling; products include food, clothes, toys, movies, and cars

target—to aim carefully at something or someone

Read More

Gaines, Ann Graham. *Master the Library and Media Center.* Ace It! Information Literacy Series. Berkeley Heights, N.J.: Enslow Publishers, 2009.

Rustad, Martha E. H. *Learning About Media Literacy.* Media Literacy for Kids. North Mankato, Minn.: Capstone Press, 2014.

Internet Sites

FactHound offers a safe, fun way to find Internet sites related to this book. All of the sites on FactHound have been researched by our staff.

Here's all you do:

Visit *www.facthound.com*

Type in this code: 9781491418307

Super-cool stuff! Check out projects, games and lots more at **www.capstonekids.com**

23

Critical Thinking Using the Common Core

How do ads target certain buyers? (Key Ideas and Details)

Look at the ad on page 9. Describe two ways it might make someone want to buy the product. (Integration of Knowledge and Ideas)

Index

Word Count: 210
Grade: 1
Early-Intervention Level: 20